5 VITAL HABITS FOR HIGH ACHIEVERS

TONY BURGESS & JULIE FRENCH
DIRECTORS OF THE ACADEMY OF HIGH ACHIEVERS (Aha!)

LEANMARKETING™
★PRESS★

First Published in Great Britain 2005
by Lean Marketing Press
www.BookShaker.com

ISBN 0 9545681 2 5

Typeset in Book Antiqua

For Wendy and Sophie

For Peter, Jez, Jenny, Molly (and Jack Black the dog)

Our wonderful families that fill our lives with magic daily

ACKNOWLEDGEMENTS

We would like to take this opportunity to acknowledge the massive support that we have received from our publishers, Lean Marketing Press.

We would also like to thank the trainers, coaches, delegates, support team and guest speakers (Sally Gunnell OBE, Joe Simpson and Chris Bonington) that made our Ignite 1 programme such a huge success. You will always have a very special place in our hearts.

We would also like to acknowledge the work of Richard Bandler and John Grinder, the co-creators of NLP (Neuro Linguistic Programming) whose work has significantly influenced our lives in so many ways.

CONTENTS

ACKNOWLEDGEMENTS

CONTENTS

FOREWORD

ASKING THE QUESTION… 1

ASPIRATION 8

ASPIRING! 18

INSPEDITION 24

EXPEDITION… I GUESS? 36

EXPEDITION 40

ONWARDS AND UPWARDS 48

ABOUT THE AUTHORS 66

THE ACADEMY OF HIGH ACHIEVERS 67

THE SUCCESS TOOLBOX 68

FOREWORD

My own research has proven that highly effective people set and achieve very large goals and NOT the much taught "realistic and achievable" goals.

Using the vowel model is a great way to help ensure that your own goals are achieved.

The A, E, I, O and U is evident in my own research and as I read these pages I recalled many top achievers that, during our interviews, have given examples of how, often without being aware of it, they have used an A and E or an O (my own personal favourite) to propel themselves towards success.

When Tony and Julie asked me to write this foreword I had mixed emotions. Having known them for a while, I wondered what plot they were scheming, as nothing is ever "just" a foreword or "just" a training event with these two.

After being a speaker at their amazing Ignite 1 event I was amongst other leading trainers and speakers that also left feeling as if they had been participants rather than trainers.

So, when I read the draft for this book I knew that it must be published for it is an invaluable aid to success.

Tony and Julie want you to understand this information, but most of all they want you to apply it, and they have this great knack of giving information in ways that are easily understood, and therefore applied.

Their "vowel" model is FANTASTIC and I urge everyone to immerse themselves in it, and then apply it to their personal lives and careers or business.

The book is a delight to read and I will refer to it often.

In our busy (and getting ever busier) lives there are pieces of information that make life easier. This book is one such piece of information.

By applying (and helping others to apply) what I have learnt from my interviews with top achievers, I (and others) have achieved so many lifetime goals in the last few years, and the principles held within these pages go a long way towards helping you to do the same.

My regret is that this book was not published many years ago.

Go on – IGNITE yourself and don't be afraid to drop your vowels, as long as you pick them up and run with them each and every time.

David Hyner

DAVID HYNER is an authority on High Achievers. He has interviewed countless highly effective people over many years and helps others to apply what he has discovered. David is a professional speaker, trainer, author and researcher.

ASKING THE QUESTION...

I loved my granddad!

You know how some people just make you feel good, just by them being in the same room as you? Well my granddad was one of those people! It didn't matter what was going on or what challenges life threw at him, he would always manage to smile through it and find a positive angle to talk about. He inspired me. He made me feel like there was always a solution to every problem. He made me realise that I could sometimes take myself and the world too seriously. He made me feel confident about my own ability to achieve things in my life – just because I know that he believed in me.

Yes, I loved my granddad!

There was something peculiar that my granddad used to say that I never got around to asking him about. And once my granddad had passed away, when I was 15 years old, it bugged me that I hadn't asked about it.

Whenever he made some kind of mistake or things didn't quite work out as he had expected he would walk in, smile and exclaim to the world, to the room, to whoever was around "Oops I dropped a vowel!"

Then he would go and sit quietly for a short time. And I could tell he was thinking. He would be concentrating like his mind was searching for the "vowel" that he had obviously let fall from his grip.

I didn't know what it was all about. And at the time I didn't have any particular urge to find out. I was happy just to notice that my granddad was working through something that he obviously found useful and he would soon be back on his feet, beaming from ear to ear with a real sense of refreshment and satisfaction like everything was now sorted out and he knew what he needed to do to make things right again.

The years went by and I became an adult with more responsibilities. From time to time I would of course face my own life challenges and at such times I would remember that image of my granddad and the sound of his voice as he said what he said – "Oops, I've dropped a vowel". "What was all that about?" I'd ask myself. Whatever it was it seemed to work for him! I sometimes wondered if it could work for me.

Looking back on it, I don't know why I didn't ask about it sooner. Maybe I liked the mystery. Maybe I wondered whether I would be able to do what he was able to do if I knew what it was all about. Maybe I just didn't have a good enough reason to go there. Who knows?

What I can tell you is that eventually I did ask. I asked my dad. I asked him at a time when I felt it was going to be really, really important to be fully prepared for anything. A time where I thought I could do with all the preparation I could get. It was at a time when my wife, Wendy had become pregnant. This was a major life step! Lots of changes on the horizon! I knew that I definitely didn't want to be 'dropping vowels' all over the place (whatever that meant!) when taking on the responsibility of raising a child!

This whole 'life change' thing was compounded by the fact that I had recently been made redundant from my job as a college lecturer and I wasn't quite sure what I was going to do next. I wasn't used to so much change all at once. If 'vowels' were good to keep hold of then I wanted to hang onto them now and I wanted to know why!

So I made the decision to ask my dad!

Dad had never really mentioned anything about my granddad's 'vowels'. In fact I wasn't sure if anyone else had even noticed what I had noticed about granddad's preoccupation with these letters!

When I asked, my dad paused and smiled as he remembered.

"Ah the vowels… the vowels…" He said, smiling warmly at the recollections that were flowing.

"What was all that about exactly?" I asked

"The vowels" he said "are the very essence of lifelong success".

"Well that sounds like it's worth a conversation about" I replied, as I got more curious.

"So why didn't you tell me about granddad's vowels before?" I asked.

"Well, I have spoken to you about this in many ways over the years, I didn't actually mention the vowels themselves to you but I have discussed the issues that they stand for. The thing is, when you were younger, you'll remember that you were not so open to taking advice from your old dad"

That was for sure – I thought I knew everything when I was younger. I didn't want to take advice from anyone. I was a stroppy teenager.

"I realised that you were not ready to take it all on board at the time" he continued "and I was so looking forward to the time when you would come to ask – you are obviously ready for this now!" he said excitedly, like he had been waiting for this conversation for a very long time.

"Well you've certainly got me intrigued" I replied "I didn't even know if you were aware of granddad's vowels."

"Oh yes. The vowels have had a very important impact on my life and your mum's too for that matter"

It turns out that mum and dad had been keeping a close watch over their own sets of vowels over the years, they just never expressed it out loud in the way that granddad did.

"So tell me then!" I demanded. "What is it all about?"

"Vowels are things that you need to keep an eye on", he said enthusiastically. "If you drop a vowel, then you really need to pick it up again quickly if you are to become and remain as successful as you want to be."

"Your granddad was a man who learned a lot in his life. He worked with some really inspirational people. He actively sought out the company of people who inspired him." dad reflected. "It was when he was in the army that he learned about the 'vowels' from one of his lifelong friends. Paul was his name. Sergeant Paul Parry to be precise. He's passed away now, many years ago. Your granddad had grown up with him and gone to school with him. Paul was someone who really inspired your granddad. I've no idea where Paul got the 'vowels' thing from or whether it was he who started the whole thing off. All I do know is that it kept them both going during the war years together and your granddad never forgot it. He was hooked. He always told me that the 'vowels' were so simple and yet so powerful. He kept them in the forefront of his mind throughout the rest of his life."

"Dad" I pleaded impatiently. "VOWELS! – Tell me what all this is actually about!"

"Right!" he said.

Dad sat down and took out a pen and some paper and began writing. As he did so, he read his words out loud.

'**A**' is for Aspiration…

'**I**' is for Inspedition…

"Hang on" I said. Surely 'E' comes next.

"Not at all" he replied. "Didn't they teach you in English lessons at school that 'i comes before e except after c'? Well I don't remember mentioning a 'c' so the 'i' must come first!

I didn't argue!

'E' is for Expedition… he continued.

'O' is for Onwards….

and

'U' is for Upwards.

"Right" I said, not feeling any wiser. "And are you going to tell me what I should make of what you have just told me?" I asked, wondering if I would ever get to know what the 'vowels' were about and wondering if I had made a mistake in asking.

"Okay, but we can't rush this", said dad.

"Take a seat and I'll talk to you about the importance of 'A' for aspiration" he said, waving me towards a chair.

I sat down, nodded and leaned forward, ready to learn.

<u>INTRODUCING THE VOWEL SYSTEM</u>

A = Aspiration

Know exactly what you want as an outcome

E = Expedition

Notice / research – Outward focus (eg what might be noticed about your external self by others, plus any available information to do with other people and the world out there)

I = Inspedition

Notice / research – Inward focus (ie what is going on within you, egs: beliefs, feelings, thoughts, expectations)

O = Onwards

Apply and rehearse what you have learned works through noticing and researching

U = Upwards

Evaluate and hone for continuous improvements

ASPIRATION

"Aspiration is where success creation begins", said dad.

"You need to have something to aspire to. Basically, you need to know what you want in life. Without knowing what you want, how are you going to make it happen?"

"If you think about it, going through life without a plan of direction is a bit like setting off on a voyage on a ship that has no rudder to steer it. You would be at the mercy of the tides, the weather and lady luck. The journey may be rough or smooth without you having any direct control and if you ever arrived at a destination, who knows whether or not it would suit you."

"If you want a smooth journey or an exciting journey or a challenging journey or a varied journey, you could make it happen if you had a plan, a compass and a rudder!"

"If features of the destination are of particular importance as well as the journey itself, then it would be wise to set off with some criteria to look out for and to compare against and you could also do some research as to where you are most likely to find such a destination and how you could most effectively get there."

"Know what you want and steer yourself towards it – that is what aspiration gives you."

"Indeed, the simple fact of clearly knowing what you want will begin to lead you towards achieving it" dad told me.

"Hmm" I replied, "I'm not sure about that last bit". "How can just knowing what you want take you there? Surely you need to actually do something?"

"Sure" he said. "And you are naturally going to be more inclined to think and act in a way that will get you what you want when you know clearly what it is that you want."

"So many people focus on what they don't want. They don't want to be poor, or they don't want to be stressed, or they don't want to be ill and so on. What will their mind be leading their thoughts, emotions and actions towards when they only seem to know clearly what they don't want? You guessed it – it will lead them exactly in the direction they want to avoid!"

"If I say to you 'don't be ill', what comes to mind?" dad asked.

"Erm, well, I supp-ose… yes… I have an image of me lying ill on my bed at home" I replied.

"Exactly."

"What do you mean, 'exactly'?" I asked.

"Well the mind starts to dwell on the very thing you don't want."

"It's like if you say to a young child 'don't touch the cake', they are likely to have their attention drawn to touching the cake – it will be playing on their mind until they touch it. If you had said 'stay over there and play like a good boy with your games' instead, it would give their mind something to focus on that would be far more likely to lead to the outcome that you are wanting to occur."

"Okay, I think I get it." I said. "So if I don't want to be poor, I should turn that around in my mind and say what I do want so that my mind starts heading in that direction – like maybe I could decide how much money I want to earn over a period of time or how much money I want to have in the bank as savings?"

"You've got it", said dad! "And that is just the start of aspiration. To get you more focused on getting what you want you need to make 'what you want' more compelling".

"What do you mean 'make it more compelling'?" I asked, not quite sure what dad was getting at.

"Well, if you want to have a certain amount in the bank by a particular time you could ask yourself some questions such as - What would it feel like to see the bank statement with those figures printed on it? Who would you celebrate with, how and where? What would it feel like to hold the cash in your hands? What would people say to you when you achieved it? And so on…"

"So you mean it is like adding detailed experiences to the desired outcomes?" I asked.

"Yes – absolutely right!"

"And another thing to do is to check for sure that it really is something that you want to achieve, so to do this you can ask yourself the question – What will achieving that goal give me?" dad suggested.

"It's a question you could ask over and over. Whenever you get an answer just ask the question again – and what will that give me and what will that give me? This drills down to what is really the thing that you desire and once you know that you will notice that there may be other possible routes to achieving what you truly want as well."

"As an example, one of my goals was to raise £100,000 for our local children's charity. As you know I am now pretty close to achieving that goal" he said. "Now at the time I set that goal I asked myself, what will raising £100,000 for our local children's charity give me? The answer that came back to me was 'a sense of achievement'. I asked myself what a sense of achievement would give me. The answer was that it would give me self-esteem – I would feel good about myself. I asked what feeling good about myself would give me and the answer was peace of mind. And so I pretty much found that what I really wanted was peace of mind. I decided that a fantastic way to get peace of mind was in fact to raise £100,000 for a charity so I stuck with my goal and it also prompted me to look at all kinds of other goals that could give me what I really wanted which was 'peace of mind'."

"As another example", he continued "your granddad went through a stage, once he had left the forces and set up his own business, where he wanted to be a millionaire. Nothing wrong with that. He was more than capable of achieving it. One day though he did a bit of work on his goal by going through the very questioning process that I have just explained. He asked what becoming a millionaire would give him and the answer was that it would get him more choices about how he spent his time. In particular, he would be able to afford to spend more time with your grandma. He asked what that would give him and the answer was that they would get to enjoy each other's company more often. He stopped asking questions at this point because he realised that he could spend more time with your grandma much easier than by becoming a millionaire. Becoming a millionaire was just one way he could free up time for her. He did not need to become a millionaire and he realised it in that moment. He spent the rest of that day working on ways that he could free up time to spend with your grandma and by the end of that day he had found an extra 9 hours a week that he could free up to spend time with her. Now if the answers to his original question – what would becoming a millionaire give him – were different he may well have decided to go for it and make himself a millionaire. It just so happened that when he realised what he really truly wanted he realised there were easier and quicker ways to make it happen."

"Another great question to ask yourself would be 'what might I lose by achieving this goal or what might I have to sacrifice to get it?' This allows you to check that you have considered fully what working towards this goal could really mean for you and this will allow you to make an informed decision as to whether to still go ahead or not."

"Right! That makes sense", I said.

"This next one is also very important", dad pointed out. "Ask yourself 'How might me achieving this goal affect other people?' Any personal change is bound to affect other people. Whenever one person changes, others will respond to the change in some way – it will affect them for sure and there may be some adjusting to be done. It is important to consider whether the impact on other people is acceptable to you or not before you begin to pursue your goal. This way you are going into your mission with your eyes wide open!"

"Okay, that seems sensible!" I said "What else?"

"Well, once you have answered all those questions and you are happy that you still want to make your goal a real outcome, you should really live it ahead of time!"

"How do you mean 'Live it'?" I asked.

"Well you know what you want, you have put in some detail and you have checked out that you really do want it to happen so why not experience it fully in your mind to make it something more real for your mind to home in on?"

"Do you mean to visualise the results like top sports people do?" I offered.

"Yep! That's exactly what I mean! If it can work for them... and it does by the way... then it will work for anyone! Visualisation is a powerful tool. Your mind experiences an imagined event just like it experiences a memory of a real situation. By visualising your success in detail you are programming your mind to accept that this is possible... no... inevitable! The more you rehearse it the better you steer your mind in the desired direction to achieve your goal! And the great thing about this is that visualising success is brilliant fun and really motivating too!"

"I can imagine it is!" I said. "So when do you do it dad?" I asked. "I've never noticed you doing any visualisation!"

"I choose my moments" He replied. "I like to sit in private where it is quiet and I can give it my full attention. I like to visualise successful outcomes just before I go to sleep at night so my mind can spend some time mulling it over when I'm asleep. I tend to have great dreams that way too! Your granddad didn't care where he did it. He could concentrate wherever he was, he just closed his eyes for a few seconds and he was away in his own world of success and happiness visualising something specific that he wanted to generate in his life."

"Yes I noticed granddad doing some weird closed eye thing – I wondered what he was doing. And it doesn't have to take ages then?" I asked, wondering where I was going to find the time for another daily task.

"Not at all! Just spend a few moments or as long as you like – it all adds impact!"

"Right" I said. "So where do I start?"

"Well, make a list of all the outcomes you would like to make happen in your life – dream big – like anything is possible - just pour it all out on a piece of paper - and then ask yourself which one jumps out at you as the most exciting goal to achieve – the one that would make the most incredible positive impact on your life by achieving it. Go with that one! And then ask the questions that will make it more compelling and will allow you to check that you do indeed want it. Once you have worked through the questions, really 'live it' in your mind and then surround yourself with images and things that will remind you day by day what it is that you are going to achieve!"

"Okay dad – that sounds wonderful but what if the outcome I want is something I don't believe I can make happen?" I asked.

"Well, we will come to beliefs later, son! You are right to ask! For now just pretend that anything is possible and ask 'HOW will I achieve this?' rather than 'CAN I achieve this? And this will steer your mind in the right direction for making it happen. If it is within the capacity of any one human being then it is certainly worth entertaining the possibility that it is within your own capabilities if you want it badly enough!"

"Okay" I said.

I admit that I struggled with his last comment a bit but dad seemed so positive about what he was telling me and he had obviously tested it over and over and found it to work for him.

"I'd better get Aspiring then" I said. "Can we talk about the other vowels tomorrow?" I asked, keen to test this aspiration stuff out as soon as I could.

"Of course" he replied. "How about at 4 o'clock after my constitutional?" My dad always had an afternoon stomp around the block to get some good fresh air into his lungs and to check his heart still had plenty of life left in it.

"I'll be here" I said and waved as I left the room, grabbed my coat and headed home.

As I walked, I realised just how long it had been since I last sat down and thought properly about what I wanted in life. This is what I needed right now. 'Aspiration!' It sounded good and it made me feel warm inside.

T<small>HOUGHTS</small> O<small>N</small> A<small>SPIRATION</small>

Know What You Want

If you don't know what you want then you're like a ship without a rudder; at the mercy of the tide, the weather and lady luck. Know what you want. Whatever voyage you choose you can make it happen if you have a destination, a compass and a rudder. Knowing what you want and why is essential.

Focus On The Positive

Focus on what you *do* want instead of what you *don't* want. Focus has power in it so be careful what you direct your attention to because you just might get a surprise if you're not careful!

Do You Really Want It?

Ask yourself the following questions to make sure that your goal is *really* what you want. The answers you get will uncover potential blocks early on. It could be that your goal needs some slight adjustment before it will work for you. Here are the questions. Pay attention to your answers.

* What might I lose by achieving this goal?
* What might I have to sacrifice to achieve this goal?
* How might achieving this goal affect other people?

ASPIRING!

When I got home, I told Wendy what dad had said about my granddad and the vowels model and the stuff about Aspiration. She could see I was excited about the whole thing, it was written all over my face.

"Have you got time for us to do some aspiring tonight Wend?", I asked her.

"Hmm, well… isn't this something that YOU want to do? You could do it and I could read my book", she said.

"Sure" I said, a little disappointed. "I thought it would be nice for me to know about your aspirations too, so that we can work together to make sure we are both getting what we want out of life – our individual goals and our shared goals."

"Hmm, now that's got me more interested. Actually, I really haven't thoroughly thought through where my life is headed for ages. I guess we have both been drifting along to some extent. Okay then, I'm up for it - after dinner we'll aspire for an hour!"

"Great!" I said. That warm feeling inside came back. "I'll go and get a notepad and some pens."

"After you have cooked dinner", she reminded me.

"Of course!" I said, turning and heading to the kitchen.

We were good at sharing the jobs at home. We worked well as a team. Sometimes Wendy was really busy and I would do more of the jobs and at other times when I was finding things hectic Wendy would take on the majority of jobs. When we were both busy we just mucked in together as best we could. I can't remember either of us ever complaining about who did what, we just got on and did stuff.

After we had demolished my speciality veggie risotto and Wendy had washed up, we sat on the settee with notepad and pens at the ready.

We made a massive list of dreams we wanted to fulfil – we really surprised ourselves. We wrote at the top of a page 'if anything is possible, then this is what will be happening in our lives in the future…' Then we just kept throwing in suggestion after suggestion after suggestion. I was hardly able to keep up with our thoughts as I scribbled everything down on the page in no particular order. Wendy's dreams were less about 'destinations' and more about 'experiences' throughout our life 'journey', whereas my goals tended to be more about clear 'milestones' and 'destinations' that we would arrive at along the way. It was weird how our minds represented things in different ways. I guess it just shows how everyone is unique.

"Wow!" said Wendy.

"Wow indeed!" I replied.

We were pretty impressed at how big we could dream and how great a life we could design for ourselves. Some of the things were personal to each of us – sometimes dreams we didn't even know that each other had. Some were to do with money, some to do with our home, some to do with time and how we spent it, some were to do with experiences and places, some were to do with business and our careers, and still more were about friends, family and giving to charity. Dad was right – this was fun!

"You know, now it is all on paper, it already seems so much more do-able than when they were just vague ideas in our heads", I said.

"Yeah" she replied "it does seem more do-able…in a scary, exciting, daunting, thrilling and unnerving kind of way!"

We laughed.

"We don't have to do them all at once!" I said. "We can choose one or a few of the goals and start taking first steps to making them happen". My geography teacher had always told us when we were a bit fazed by the size of the projects we were being set that the way to eat an elephant was 'one bite at a time!'

We decided to choose an individual goal each and a shared goal to work on. We spent the rest of the evening (far longer than an hour in the end because we got so into it) working through those questions that added flesh to the bones and made sure that we really wanted those outcomes (we found that we did, even though there would be some changes to our routines and things we might lose by making our goals happen).

We ended our aspiration session by spending ten minutes quietly relaxing and visualising the goals as if they had already happened. We really enjoyed it. We played some relaxing music low in the background and we were amazed how much detail we could bring to mind as we relaxed more and let go of any thoughts about whether or not we were doing it right. We had initially stopped after the first minute and found ourselves questioning whether we were doing it in the correct way because both of us were only getting hazy pictures. We decided that we were trying too hard and that we should simply go with the flow and let ourselves dream in whatever way worked for us. Once we accepted that there wasn't a 'right' way to do it except whichever way worked for us, the images and feelings and even sounds flowed so much easier, sometimes it was really detailed and at other times it was less detailed – it didn't matter at all to us. It felt more natural this way and it really was compelling.

When I opened my eyes, I felt so refreshed and energised and yet deeply calm inside at the same time.

"That was great!" said Wendy, "Its like I'm already there."

"We should definitely do this more often" I said.

"I'm going to start visualising every morning before I begin the day", she proclaimed.

"Right", I said, "Well I reckon I'm going to choose to do it late on in the evening before I go off to sleep. Dad said that works well for him and I like the idea of dreaming about these positive outcomes all night!"

"So what's next?" asked Wendy.

"Well let's plan what we are going to actually DO to begin to make these things happen starting today", I said (with surprising commitment).

Wendy yawned. "Well I'm going to start tomorrow" she said. She was looking happy and tired and was making me yawn too. We put the notepad in a prominent position on the shelf in the living room and headed off to bed.

"Have sweet dreams" said Wendy as she plumped up her pillow and then turned off the light.

"I plan to!" I replied as I snuggled into the duvet.

If Anything Is Possible, Then...

Write a list of all the outcomes and things you might like to happen in your life. Dream big and bold. Brainstorm every idea that comes into your head. Just pour it all out onto the page. In fact, if you have a close partner, then do it together.

1. Get a large sheet of paper and some pens together
2. In the centre of your page write the following phrase...
   "If Anything Is Possible Then This Is What Will Be Happening In My/Our Life In The Future"
3. Now surround this statement with all your wildest and biggest dreams and ideas. Think about all aspects of your life while doing it. Get brainstorming!

Make It Compelling

Once you're done brainstorming choose one thing that really jumps out at you. Then start visualising what success means. Live the success ahead of time. Do this every time you feel like it. Just before you go to sleep every night is a powerful time. Here are some guidelines for visualising your success.

1. Use all your senses.
2. Ask yourself, "What will achieving this give me?" then ask again, "And what will *that* give me?" and again, "And what will *that* give me?" keep going.

INSPEDITION

"Hi Dad!" I said as I let myself into the house.

"Hi son!" he replied and I noticed that he was already sat at the table with a notepad and pen ready for our meeting to start.

"Inspedition" he said, as I took a seat next to him "is all about inner discovery".

"Discovery of what?" I asked

"Discovery of what things are like inside when you are at your best, performing brilliantly, getting the outcomes you want! If you want more of that then it pays to find out as much about that as possible, don't you think?" he said in an all-knowing kind of voice.

"Yes, I guess so. But what kind of 'inner' things would I focus on?" I asked, a little confused.

"Well what goes on inside you that you can turn your attention to?"

"Erm... feelings and emotions?"

"That's a good start", said dad leaving a pointed pause, I guess so that I would continue to offer more suggestions.

"And... perhaps... erm... thoughts?" I asked

He nodded and waited.

"And beliefs and expectations?" I offered.

"Mm-hmm" he affirmed.

"And organs and blood and intestines" I said, gaining momentum.

"Whoa there!", he cut in, "This is starting to get messy. Lets stick with the ones you've already said – Thoughts, feelings, emotions, expectations, beliefs!"

"Okay" I said, feeling that I'd overstepped the mark.

"So what might you notice about your thoughts when things are going great, you are performing well and you are getting the outcomes that you have aspired to?" He asked.

There was a long pause.

"Hmm, this is not as easy as I thought it might be" I said. "I am not used to thinking about my thinking!"

"Just say whatever occurs to you" dad told me.

"Well I suppose that there are differences – I just don't seem to be able to put my finger on them!"

"Luckily you don't have to put your finger on them, you simply need to notice them. Let's do an experiment", he suggested.

"Okay" I replied, curious about what would come next.

"Allow a situation to come to mind where you were performing brilliantly, where things were going really well, where you just knew that you were on 'top form' getting the outcome that you wanted. Let such a situation just bubble to the surface of your mind now."

There was a short pause.

"Got one?" He asked.

"Yes got one!" I replied.

"Okay. Now close your eyes!" He instructed. "Be in that situation now, in that body, looking through those eyes, hearing through those ears, feeling what you feel."

"I'm there", I said. I had brought to mind a college lesson I had taught that had gone particularly well where the students were fully engaged, learning well and also enjoying the experience.

"Good. Now let's get into some of the detail of how you are representing the situation. If your mind has a screen – let's refer to it as your mind's eye – tell me, is the picture filling all of the space on the screen that is your mind's eye or is it filling just part of the available space?"

"Well I wouldn't have noticed without you asking but it seems to be filling about three quarters of the available space and it is slightly over to the right – how strange!" I reported.

"Good" said dad. "And remember, there are no right answers here – everyone is unique so just report what is going on for you – this is just discovery."

"Right!" I said, eager to continue.

"And now tell me – is the picture in colour or in black and white?"

"Colour" I said.

"And does it have movement or is it like a snapshot – almost like a photo?"

"It is moving like a film" I replied.

"And is it clear and sharp or hazy and blurred?" He asked.

"Pretty clear" I said.

"Great. And is the picture close up or far away?"

"Close."

"Can you see you in the picture, like you are looking at the scene from the outside? Or is it like you are fully there in the scene experiencing what you experience from inside your body?"

"I'm actually in there – I am seeing through my eyes in that situation. Blimey, I would not have noticed all that if you had not drawn my attention to it. We really don't think about how we think do we?" I said.

"Up until now you haven't and it is really useful to do so from now on. Now, let me ask you some more questions."

"Fire away" I said.

"Is there any sound?"

"Hmmm, I would say no – no sound is there. Is that right? Is that okay?" I asked a bit disturbed.

"Remember what I said. There are no right answers! This is just discovery as to how your mind represents things when things are going well! No two people are exactly the same so just go with whatever comes to mind. It will be useful" He reassured me.

"Okay. Well I noticed no sound."

"And in that situation, right there, right now, tell me about any thinking voice you may be thinking in."

"Thinking voice?" I asked and then immediately knew what he meant. I paused for a few moments to allow my self-talk to flow.

"Well I am saying to myself 'this is going well'. I'm saying to myself 'great job!'"

"And what kind of voice are you thinking in?" dad prompted. "Is it loud or quiet, high pitched or low pitched or somewhere in between? Is your voice coming from in front of you or behind you or to the left or the right or maybe from above or below? Notice it all!" dad told me.

"Okay. Well it seems to be coming from behind me, close behind me. It is a loud and confident voice. A happy and motivated voice. It is encouraging and reassuring. I had always thought my thinking voice would have been pretty much the same all the time but it isn't. This voice is just like the kind of voice I would use if I was congratulating someone on a job well done and wanting them to keep it up".

"Great", said dad, "and now I want you to notice any feelings you have inside, in that situation right now. Tell me what you feel and where that feeling starts".

"Oh, well, I have... erm... well..."

"Just say what comes to mind", Said dad patiently.

"It's… a good feeling…"

"What is a good feeling like and where does it begin?"

"It's… it's a light feeling… it's a feeling like there is an elevator inside my tummy that is slowly lifting easily and effortlessly… it sounds crazy I know but you did say to just say what comes to mind!" I said, a bit embarrassed.

"That's good" dad replied. I felt relieved.

"And what are your beliefs in that moment that you are becoming increasingly aware of?"

"My beliefs? Erm… My beliefs!… The beliefs that spring to mind are that I am capable and effective at teaching and that if I can get this kind of response once I can do it more often. I am also believing that these students want to learn and are willing to put effort in because they are enjoying themselves."

"Good!" Said dad. "And what expectations do you have in that situation right now?"

"My expectations… Hmm… My expectations are… that the students will retain the material well today and that I will walk out of this lesson feeling good about myself and the students in the class"

"Okay. Good. And now open your eyes" dad instructed me.

I opened my eyes, a little surprised about how much detail I had noticed about my inner experiences that I had not noticed before.

"You see it can be easy to notice how we think and feel when we set time aside to do it and we have the intention to discover what is working. Now we need something to compare it to", said dad.

"Like what?" I asked.

"Like some time when things were not going so well. Where you would have liked things to have been better and would like things to be better in the future."

"Okay" I said "What about the times when I walk into a new situation and don't know anyone and I feel a bit isolated or awkward?"

"That will do perfectly for this exercise" my dad replied.

We then spent a few minutes, me with my eyes closed having allowed an appropriate situation to come to mind and dad with a whole series of prompting questions at the ready to get me to notice detail of the experience of being there.

I found it easier this time. I had the idea of what I could notice and I noticed quickly with hardly any prompt at all.

There were some interesting differences between the way I experienced the first situation where things were going great and the second situation where things were going less well.

One of the main differences was that when I was experiencing myself in a situation where I was confident I was seeing the picture over to the right slightly whereas when I was experiencing myself in a situation where I was feeling nervous and awkward I was seeing the picture over to the left in my mind's eye. I also noticed that there were major differences in my thinking voice in the two situations and my feelings were very different in each situation.

"We can of course get into even more detail on this exercise" Dad told me. "We could get into detail like what you can taste or smell in each situation, we can get into the sizes of things and people in the situation, the textures of the things around you – the more you do this kind of exercise, the more you notice!"

"Right!" I said, convinced that this was true because I had been surprised at how much detail I had noticed already.

"So what exactly do we do with this detail that we have discovered?" I asked.

"Well the simple answer is that you will do more of whatever works for you! Do more of the thinking and feeling and mental representing that gets you the outcomes that you want. Now, I'm due to help your mother with some tasks. Let's carry on tomorrow evening. I'd like you to do some expedition next."

"Expedition?" I asked "Wait, let me guess – discovery with an outward focus?!"

"You got it!" dad replied. "See you tomorrow – will 7 o'clock be alright?"

"Can we make it 8?" I asked. I had some errands to run.

"Sure. 8 o'clock it is then."

"Great."

I left for home and my mind was wondering what else I had been missing as I had been going through life. So much information that could be useful to me I had not been noticing until now!"

I talked for hours with Wendy when I got home. We also began planning things we would start to do to make our aspirations into realities. There were things we could begin to do that very week.

My mind was still discovering what works when I turned off the light and went off to sleep.

GO ON AN INSPEDITION...

When you go on an inspedition you'll go inside yourself to see what you can actively notice about your experience. Knowing the little differences between when you're at your best and when you'd like to be better will give you valuable clues in building your achievement potential.

In particular you'll be allowing yourself to notice:
- Sights
- Sounds
- Feelings (physical and emotional)
- Thoughts
- Beliefs
- Expectations

WHAT DO YOU NOTICE?

The following exercise will help you to really notice what's going on inside you. It calls for you to close your eyes so you may want to remember it, get a friend to coach you or even record yourself reading this out loud and play it back.

Allow a situation to come to mind when you were truly operating at your very best. Let such a situation simply bubble to the surface of your mind <u>now</u>...

Close your eyes. Be in that situation right now. Experience it fully. Looking through those eyes. Hearing with those ears. Feeling whatever you're feeling.

Good. Now let's get into some of the detail of how you are representing the situation. If your mind has a screen – let's refer to it as your mind's eye – notice, is the picture filling all of the space on the screen that is your mind's eye or is it filling just part of the available space?"

Good. Remember, there are no right answers here – everyone is unique so just notice what is going on for you – this is just discovery.

Now notice...

Is the picture in colour or in black and white?

Does it have movement – like a movie or is it like a snapshot – almost like a photo. Is it clear and sharp or hazy and blurred? Close up or far away? Can you see yourself in the picture, like you are looking at the scene from the outside? Or is it like you are fully there in the scene experiencing what you experience from inside your own body?

Now listen. Is there any sound? Remember - there are no right answers! Your experience is uniquely yours. No two people are exactly the same so just go with whatever comes to mind. It will be useful.

And in that situation, right there, right now, notice any thinking voice you may be thinking in. If it's present notice what it's saying. What kind of voice are you thinking in? Is it loud or quiet, high pitched or low pitched, fast or slow? Or somewhere in between? Is your voice coming from in front of you or behind you or to the left or the right or maybe from above or below?

Notice it all!

Now notice any feelings you have inside, in that situation right now. Notice what you feel and where that feeling is. Where it starts...

Just feel...

That's right...

Now... what beliefs in that moment are you becoming increasingly aware of?

Good...

Now... what expectations do you have in that situation right now?

Okay. Good. Now open your eyes.

Once you've completed the above exercise write down what you discovered. You'll now need another experience to compare it to. Think of a time when you'd have liked things to be better. If 10 was fantastic and 0 was awful choose an experience that you'd consider a 5 or 6. Now do the exercise all over again with this new experience. Then compare your notes.

EXPEDITION... I GUESS?

"Your dad is in bed with a bad head", my mum's voice said down the telephone at 7:45 in the evening.

"Oh" I said, concerned and also disappointed "Whose bad head is he in bed with?" I joked.

"Very funny. Your dad just had a little too much whiskey last night I think. After you had left yesterday, we had Tom and Mavis round from next-door showing us their holiday snaps – we always end up drinking late when they come round. It was a great evening and your dad is well and truly paying for it now."

"Right" I said as I thought to myself how selfish dad had been to ruin any chance of any expedition that evening. Funny how your perceptions can be so biased when something you want is being delayed. In fact it was becoming clearer and clearer to me that everything we perceive has a bias – that the only reality is the one we create for ourselves at any given moment – some of it is useful and some of it is not so useful. My inspedition had made me very much aware of that!

Mum informed me, "Your dad said that you should take the opportunity to go out and 'people watch'. He said you should go somewhere where you would find people who you admire and think are worth looking into."

"Did he say what I should be looking for?" I asked, a little frustrated that I was being set a task with so little guidance.

"He just said to notice everything that is useful" she replied.

"Well that narrows it down" I thought out loud. And then remembered what dad had said when we were doing inspedition – there were no right and wrong answers – it was just discovery.

"Thanks mum! Did dad say when we could meet up again?" I asked.

"Hang on a second" Her voice became a distant yell as she called my dad and asked him when we could meet again. I am sure I heard a groan and a mumbled response about asking more quietly and a few seconds later my mum returned to the phone and said "He could see you at eight tomorrow evening if that suits you. Hopefully he will be in a better mood by then."

"Okay mum. Thanks. Tell him I'll see him at eight tomorrow then. You look after yourself. See you soon. Bye."

"Bye."

I told Wendy what my task was and she suggested that we go somewhere together.

"Great. Where shall we go?" I asked.

"Let's go to the comedy club", she suggested, "I have always found it really admirable how confident and creative people can be on stage when they are performing. That has got to be worth looking into!"

I too admired the confidence that many performers showed when they got on stage and I was fascinated by how some performers could hold an audience's attention so fully that a packed room could be howling with laughter one moment and perfectly silent the next at the whim of the performer.

"Yes, you are right – that has to be worth looking into."

We spent a very enjoyable evening together at the club, soaking up the atmosphere and enjoying the entertainment. This time we were enjoying it in a new way. We were more fully engaged and appreciative of the detail of the performances. We noticed all kinds of things about the performers, particularly the differences we could notice between the best performers and those who were getting less of a response from the audience. We also noticed details about members of the audience – we focused mainly on the differences between those who seemed relaxed and comfortable and those who seemed to be more self-conscious. Also, because of our recent inspeditions we also noticed more about our own inner responses too – we knew the information could be useful to us later.

PEOPLE WATCHING

1. Find an opportunity to observe a person or people who have a high level of ability in a certain skill or behaviour that you might like to have too.

2. Describe for your own benefit, specifically, what it is you admire about their ability and write this down.

3. Watch what they do, noticing anything and everything that's useful. Notice as specifically as possible what's really working for them.

4. Write down what you've noticed that might be useful.

EXPEDITION

"Hi son!" said dad I as I let myself into my parents house at 7:55.

Dad was looking a bit embarrassed.

"Hi dad" I said, smirking.

"Your inspedition didn't tell you it was time to stop drinking then?" I asked mischievously.

"Not this time!" He replied. "The vowels don't make you perfect you know. I dropped a vowel last night – In fact I dropped two of them. I dropped my aspiration – the outcome I wanted for the evening - and I dropped my inspedition – I did not pay attention to the fact that I enjoyed my third whiskey better than my fourth and fifth and sixth, ahem, and seventh".

"You paid for that slip up then", I said with a chuckle.

"Let's move on", he said with a smile.

"How did you get on with your expedition last night?" he asked.

"Well I'm not sure if we were doing what you expected us to do but we certainly did some noticing. We went to the comedy club and watched some performers and the audience in detail – I have to say it was fascinating to watch with the extra agenda to notice what is working and what may be useful"

"So what kinds of things did you notice on your expedition?" he asked curiously.

"Well we picked up a lot of information about the performers' body language, facial expressions, their posture, the speed at which they talked and moved, the tone and volume of their voices, how much they varied their voices and so on" I reported. "There were quite a number of similarities between those who gave the best performances on the night – they do things differently to those who gave less effective performances."

"Bravo! That is a great piece of expedition, son. Well done! And did you enjoy it?" he asked.

"Yes I did actually. It made us realise just how much information there is out there that could be useful. I feel like if I wanted to be a great comedian or performer, there were lots of things I could adopt that would make me more effective. I guess the more detail I take the time to notice, the more I would be able to replicate what is clearly working for others?" I speculated.

"You really are catching on to this vowels stuff aren't you?", said dad smiling, "And there is more you can discover through expedition too".

"Expedition is discovery with an outward focus – beyond your own inner world. You have already used your senses to notice what is working for other people. You can also take things a step further by asking questions when you make the opportunities to do so. For example, if you wanted to be more confident in a particular social situation, you could of course listen to and observe people who are already effectively 'doing

41

confidence' in that social situation just as you listened to and observed performers in the comedy club. You could also ask questions of one or more of those people who are effectively 'doing confidence' and find out what they are doing in terms of their thinking and their emotions. This can seem unusual to them at first but once you tell them that you regard them as an example of excellence they tend to be pretty happy to report what they can to help you."

"So what about if the person who is doing something particularly effectively is a celebrity or someone I am unlikely to meet or speak to?" I asked.

"Well lots can be learned by making a point of watching them being interviewed or by reading their biography and in fact don't assume that you cannot meet or speak to them just because they are wealthy, successful or famous. Your granddad made a real point of getting to speak to some of the people he thought were most worth looking into – most of them were sports people and business people and he had a pretty good hit rate in terms of getting to ask them questions. Sometimes it took a long time, sometimes it took cheek and ingenuity and it often got him what he wanted."

"Okay" I said, surprised to hear that my granddad had been so proactive in pursuing his heroes. "And what kinds of questions might I ask?"

"Whatever helps you to understand the detail of what they are doing inside" dad told me. "If you wonder what it is like to think in a confident way when in a particular situation you can ask the kinds of questions I asked you the other day – for example, what beliefs do they have that are useful? What are they expecting? What is the thinking voice in their head like? And so on. Like I said they find it a bit weird at first to be asked such questions – just like you found it a bit weird yourself - and most will be flattered to have so much interest shown in their success and will then respond positively. Of course, excellence is all around us and there are friends and family and colleagues and associates that we can ask questions of whenever we want to understand how they are doing what they do best. You don't need to speak to the famous to find out what works – just find people who are doing some particular thing more effectively than you and go into discovery mode."

"That makes sense" I replied. And it really did. Everywhere I went I would be able to notice examples of success that could be useful to explore.

"And this sounds time consuming", I said.

"It only need be as time consuming as is useful to you" he replied like an all knowing, all wise sage.

"Right!" I said

"You can just fine tune your senses and notice more as you go through your life. You don't need to be asking people questions all the time, only when it suits you to know even more detail to achieve something that is particularly important to you." He told me.

"Okay. So is there anything else involved in this whole expedition business?" I asked.

"Sure. Anything about YOU that is available as useful information on the outside is also worth discovering and this would also be referred to as expedition. So for example, if you wanted to be an excellent comedian you might want to film yourself performing so that you have all of the 'outward' signs available to you as to what is and what is not working. You might want to ask other people who know you or have experienced you in particular situations to give you feedback about what they have picked up in terms of what you do that works. A good example of this is when someone tells you 'well done' for something, you could take a few moments to really get into the detail of what they think worked well. Ask them 'what specifically was it that had impact on you and led you to congratulate me?' and then take careful note of what they tell you."

"So there is more to self-discovery than what is happening on the inside?" I asked.

"Yes, self-discovery is a mix of inspedition and expedition – for best results do both!" dad replied.

"Well I reckon I understand expedition alright. It will take a bit of practise and it might seem strange to ask the questions at first but it does all make sense. It's all about finding and adding more and more pieces to our jigsaws of success until everything becomes clear, isn't is?" I said, quite pleased with my jigsaw metaphor.

"You are sounding more like your granddad each day" he replied and I got a warm feeling inside my tummy that let me know that the pieces were slotting into place.

"Dad I feel like I know what I need to do now. As I have been discovering what works I have found myself experimenting with doing more of what works, like I have been deliberately thinking in a voice that makes me feel good more often and adjusting my posture for creating a confident state and so on. Is this what I should be doing?"

"That is exactly what you should be doing, son! In the vowels system we call it 'Onwards' – it is where you apply more of what works to get more of the outcomes you desire. You will automatically want to do more of what works as you discover it and so you are right not to wait. The vowels system is not a linear process where you need to do one vowel process then the next then the next. Although your aspirations need to be pretty clear first to be most effective, the remaining vowels processes would be done in parallel. So you may be out and about noticing what is working on the outside and the inside whilst keeping particular desired outcomes in mind and experimenting with testing out what works as you discover it. All of this in combination becomes second nature after a while. When a person first starts using the vowels system they sometimes find it useful to concentrate on one vowel process at a time until they get used to doing it. Others get into using all the vowel processes in combination very quickly. I suspect you will be one of those people."

"Really? And what specifically did you notice that told you that I would be quick to catch onto this?" I asked smugly.

"Your smugness!" he replied with his eyes sparkling.

"Tomorrow we will cover Onwards and Upwards and then you will have the whole system" he told me. "Can you be here at ten tomorrow morning? As it is Saturday, your mum has a shopping trip planned in the afternoon and I am going to accompany her."

"I'll check what Wendy has planned and I'll phone you later" I replied and picked up my coat and headed for the door "Thanks dad!" I said. "It is all coming together". I gave him a hug and then my mum came through to say goodbye and to give me a hug too.

"See you both tomorrow", I said

"Bye" they chorused as they waved me off.

Discovery With An Outward Focus

An expedition is discovery with an outward focus. Simply watching people "doing" a desired behaviour (such as being confident, gaining rapport, persuading, performing etc.) can provide you with an enormous amount of information that you can apply to your own achievement. You can also get an external perspective on the things you already do well or would like to improve. Both offer you a wealth of evidence you can use to improve.

Get Out There And Find Out What's Going On For Them

When you find people who are really proficient at performing a particular behaviour it can be extremely beneficial to find out more about their "internal workings" too. Simply ask questions that will give you whatever helps you understand. Some ideas:

- How are they thinking?
- How are their feelings being experienced?
- What useful beliefs do they hold?
- What are they expecting?
- What is their thinking voice saying? How does it sound?
- Are they making or recalling pictures? What are they like?

ONWARDS AND UPWARDS

In fact it was Sunday before I saw them again because Wendy had reminded me that we had arranged to visit friends out of town on the Saturday.

Wendy and I had come over to mum and dad's for Sunday lunch and it was early afternoon over coffee that dad and I began to talk about the vowels system again.

"Onwards…" dad began "…as I said to you before, is about applying what you have discovered works to get more of the outcomes that you want." he summarised. "You have already said that you have been adopting certain physical postures that you know make you feel more confident and you have been changing the voice in your head to create certain emotional states. This is easier than most people think isn't it?" he asked.

"Well I must admit, I did not think that changing my posture, facial expression and degree of muscle tension and so on would have so much impact so quickly on how I feel. It is so simple and yet so effective. I suppose most of the most powerful ideas and techniques are often the simplest ones. Also the voice in the head thing – a few days ago I was not really even aware that the voice in my head changed in different situations let alone that I could change that voice at will. I have found that, for me, changing my thinking voice is one of the best tools for getting me into appropriate states of mind quickly. Especially when I combine it with the right physiology. When I think in a confident and motivated voice and stand tall and look up and bring my shoulders back and speak louder I feel awesome within just a few moments." I reported.

"Good. And there is more you can do to intensify that too" Dad told me. "You know when you get that good feeling inside as you stand tall and think in that voice?"

"Yes" I said. I could feel the start of it just by remembering it.

"Well how would it be if you could turn up that feeling to whatever level you want so that you can feel as great as you want when you want?"

"Now that would be brilliant!" I said.

"Well it is easier than you ever imagined!" He told me. "For some people it simply involves imagining a control dial like there is for turning up the volume on a music system, a dial that you can just turn up to full and as you do so the feeling inside gets turned right up with it. For other people they imagine the good feeling spinning around inside, bigger and faster until it takes over the whole of their body. There are loads of personal development techniques for triggering and turning up good feelings. Remember you told me that a good feeling that you have feels like an elevator inside?"

"Yes I remember" I said and immediately got that good feeling inside.

"Well what if you close your eyes now..." I closed my eyes.

"…And you imagine how that elevator looks."

"Yes" I said, picturing it clearly.

"Now double the size of that elevator… and let it rise quicker… followed by another elevator and another one, each one bigger than the last… How does that feel?" he asked.

"Whoa!" I said. "You should bottle that! That feels great inside."

"And everyone has their own particular way of turning up a good feeling – it is great fun experimenting and playing until you find one that works spectacularly well! For me it is a giant merry-go-round on its side spinning clockwise and powered by rockets!" He told me and as he spoke I could tell he was becoming more energised.

"They should teach this stuff in schools", I said.

"There are lots of things that should be taught in schools that are not" he replied.

"You know how we compared how you pictured things in your head when things were going well and when they were going not so well?" he asked.

"Yes"

"Again, to do more of what works, simply notice what features are key to a particular positive representation, such as confidence or certainty or motivation and then add them in to any picture where it would be useful to have such a positive representation. For example, you found that when you were representing something you were confident about, you tended to see it over to the right, whereas when you were representing something where you felt low levels of confidence it was pictured over to the left."

"I remember that!" I confirmed

"Well a great example of 'Onwards' that comes from that bit of 'inspedition' would be to move the representation of your low confidence situation from the left over to the right. Do it now and see what happens."

I closed my eyes. I pictured a scene where I had felt awkward walking into a room full of people I didn't know. It was over to the left as before.

"How do I move it?" I asked.

"However seems best to you" Dad replied "You could have the picture on wheels and wheel it over to the right. Or you could have an army of ants carry it over. Or you could just give it a mental nudge over there, or fire it from a cannon or whatever works for you."

I thought for a second and then gave a mental nudge (whatever that is!) that moved the picture over to the right of my mind's eye. It was easy and more to the point it worked. It felt much better to have the picture over there on the right. I actually felt more confident about the situation when it was pictured on the right. "How bizarre" I thought. And then I realised that all I had done was match the features of what I knew made me feel confident. It made a lot of sense to me.

"That works!" I said.

"And what about beliefs dad?" I asked "surely I can't just drop certain beliefs and take on new ones just because they would work better for me?"

"I've done it many, many times son!" he replied. "Again, this is easier than you think. All beliefs are just ways of making sense of the world. Once you accept that any belief is just as valid as another and some happen to work better and more positively than others, you can chop and change beliefs to suit the outcomes you want to achieve. Of course, just like a well-practised behaviour, some beliefs will seem very familiar and newer ones may seem a little awkward at first. The way I adopt a new belief when I know it works well for others is to act 'as if' I truly believed the new belief."

"You mean you don't actually believe it fully straight away?" I asked.

"Sure" he replied. "As an example, when I went for a job interview a few years ago, I knew who else was going to be interviewed and I believed that the others were better candidates for the job. They had worked at the place for much longer than me and although I knew that I had everything that was needed to do the job exceptionally well I had the unhelpful belief that I was not up to it in the same way that they were. I believed that length of time working for the company was a clear indicator of suitability for the job. This belief was going to get in the way of my success. I had a clear outcome in mind.

I wanted this job. So I decided that a more useful belief would be that I was equally suitable for the job as the other candidates and that the interview panel had other criteria in mind that were far more important than number of years with the company.

I imagined what it would be like to walk into the interview room with that new belief and it felt better. So then I wondered what it would be like to go in with a belief that I was the very best candidate for the position and that all the criteria that the interviewers were using to make a selection were exactly the ones that made me most favourable. I imagined what it would be like to go into interview with that new belief and I felt so much more confident and focused on what I was going to say to sell myself on my best points.

This imagination of going through the situation with a newly adopted belief in place was like having a testing ground that was giving me feedback that made the belief more real to me. I mentally rehearsed having that belief over and over and the results were so good that the belief became real by the time I went into the interview. Even if I had only partially adopted the belief by the time of the interview, it would be far better for me to go in 'as if' I believed I was the best candidate than to go in believing I was the underdog."

"And you got the promotion so it must have worked" I said

"Yes it did and the belief was strengthened by the results that came" He replied.

"And what if you had not got the job?" I asked.

"Well that was never an option to me in my mind when I went into the interview" He said "And if the outcome had been that I was not offered the job I could choose to believe whatever I wanted. I could choose to believe that I was in fact the underdog, I could choose to believe that I was the best candidate and did not give my best performance on the day, I could choose to believe that the interview panel had made a terrible mistake or whatever. The belief I would have chosen would be the one that served me best when I tested them out."

"Okay" I said thoughtfully. "Choosing beliefs is a bit of a strange concept though isn't it? I had always accepted that beliefs take years to develop and would take an equally long period of experience to change."

"I do not expect for you to take what I am saying on board without having tested it out" Dad told me. "Just test it for yourself and when it works for you then you can accept it".

"That sounds reasonable" I said.

"It is!" he replied, smiling.

"So what about moving onwards in terms of applying what I have discovered through expedition?" I enquired.

"Same thing applies" He said "Just adopt whatever you notice works!"

"Like when I noticed particular patterns to the way the most successful comedians performed?" I asked.

"Exactly. Just take on board what they are doing that seems to be working and test it out for yourself. Incorporate what works for them into your own repertoire of behaviours and see what happens. If it works for you, keep it. If it doesn't, go back into discovery mode until you hit the one that works for you."

"And If I asked someone about the beliefs and thoughts and feelings that they had when they were operating at their best would I then just test those beliefs, thoughts and feelings out on myself – 'as if' I had already made them part of my repertoire?" I asked.

"Sure. That would work. And the more detail you can get from them the more easily you will be able to reproduce what they are doing inside." He replied. "And don't forget that you can respond to the detailed feedback that others give you about your outward behaviours. Do more of what they tell you has the impact and see if it gets you better results."

"Makes sense" I said.

"Sometimes it may be useful for you to test out a person's whole identity if they are getting results that you want for yourself. You could ask yourself, who do I need to *be* to achieve x? Usually someone will easily come to mind who is already achieving x spectacularly well and you could borrow their identity for a while to see how it works for you. In other words you could go about activities related to achieving x 'as if' you were that other person in every way, with their beliefs, their behaviours, their posture and so on and notice what works particularly well and decide what you want to integrate into your own identity.

I have stolen the identities of many people in my life and 'me' as I know it has all kinds of features that I have kept from other successful people. I switch on those features whenever it suits me best. So many people see themselves as being helpless victims of their personality traits when it can be so easy to test out and adopt new ones. I don't know about you – I prefer to be in control of my identity!"

"Sounds better than being a victim!" I replied, acutely aware that I had on many an occasion previously blamed my personality or some other aspect of my identity for past failures. At that very moment I was inspired to no longer be a victim or to use such excuses for not getting the outcomes I wanted.

"Son, you know there are so many ways that you can take on board the excellence that you discover through expedition and inspedition and I keep finding new ways the more I play. That is the beauty with the vowels system. It is so flexible and allows you to experiment and to get creative. Just play and discover and apply whatever works for you and you will just keep on improving! Of course, there are a wealth of excellent personal development training programmes that you can go on that give you new tools and techniques that allow you to discover and apply what works. Your granddad was constantly adding to his success toolbox and he went on some great training programmes and also some very poor ones. The key is to not get rigid and serious about it all or adopt too many rules.

Personal development should be creative, flexible and fun and the vowels system is simply a useful framework by which you can check that you are covering all the important bases with your tools and techniques."

"Right" I said. "So you mean that this is just the beginning for me in terms of my personal development?"

"Yes!" he replied. "Isn't that exciting? Your granddad never stopped developing in his lifetime and I do not intend to stop during mine. In my view a person is always either stagnating or declining if they stop improving, and I reckon carrying on improving is the best bet for a successful and fulfilling life."

"Hmm. Don't fancy stagnation or decline much" I said. "Continuous improvement definitely sounds more appealing."

Dad went to get more coffee.

When he returned he began to speak again immediately.

"Upwards" he said "Is simply to remind you to do an evaluation of what you've applied, then you can weed out what doesn't work and hone what does work"

"So it is kind of a checking and tweaking process?" I asked.

"Yes it is just that. It makes good sense to check whether something new is working for us or not. If it isn't we may need to tweak it to make it work and to do this we would need to return to inspedition and expedition to check out what details we may have missed. It may be that even after tweaking the new way of doing things we are not getting the expected improvements and if this is the case we might choose to drop that new behaviour in favour of a new experiment in discovering and testing out what works.

Of course when something works well for us we might want to find ways to make it work even better for us through tweaking the detail. So for example, if thinking in a loud and confident voice makes you feel really confident, maybe you might tweak that thinking voice by turning the volume up even louder and making it sound even more confident to see what effect that has on you. The great thing about this is that if it works it has led to a rapid improvement, if it does not make a difference then you can reverse it just as easily."

"I will test out tweaking my thinking voice for sure because it has had such an impact on me so far" I said.

"Well the same applies for all things that work. If for example a person finds that shrinking down the mental image they have of something they find scary works in terms of reducing their fear of that thing then they could shrink it some more so it is the size of a pin head and then they could imagine flicking it away like a speck of dust. Or if distorting the image in comical ways works best, then they could make it more funny and ridiculous. So someone who is scared of public speaking might imagine their audience with party hats on to make them seem less threatening. If that works for them they might choose to exaggerate the distortion and imagine them all in full fancy dress to see if that makes them seem even less threatening and more comical – they can always reverse it if it has no additional effect."

"You do come up with some bizarre ideas dad!" I said.

"That's true. And I have found that often the more bizarre, ridiculous and comical the technique is the more useful it turns out to be, particularly when removing an unhelpful fear" he replied. "And it means you can really let your imagination run riot – it really is great fun you know!"

"I'm seeing a side of you that I never suspected was even there", I said. "I must have been crazy not to have listened when you tried to talk to me about these tools when I was younger."

"You just weren't ready", he replied. "Different people are ready to receive and adopt these tools at different times – when you were younger you thought you already had all the tools you needed. As you have said, some of this stuff is pretty bizarre and you would have found the vowels system hard to accept at the time."

"If it works, it works!" I said with conviction.

"Yes and we really should do more of whatever works. I am glad you asked me about the vowels, son. I know that using the system will work well for you. Your granddad would be pleased to know that you are going to benefit from the system!"

"Good old granddad!" I proclaimed out loud.

"Thanks for talking me through the system Dad!" I said with real feeling "It came at a very good time for me."

"Funny how we find the solutions we need once we know what we want and start to look in the right places" said dad in what has since become known as his 'sage voice'.

"It has been a real pleasure to teach someone about the vowels. I haven't done that in ages. It has helped to reinforce it for myself too. When I was a senior manager before I retired I used to share the system a lot with my team and the other managers and directors. It was a great structure to give to the people I was coaching within the company – although of course they didn't call it coaching in those days. You know, you should find someone to teach this system to as soon as possible to help reinforce it in your own mind" he suggested.

"I've been working through the system with Wendy" I told him. "And you are right – it does help! I will definitely share this with others too – they can't help but benefit from this if they open their mind to it. Like I said they should teach this in schools."

"Surely with your education links you could make it part of the compulsory curriculum!" he said with a smile.

"Now that really would be a mission!" I said, again with a broad smile, partly because I would love to see the system and all the personal development that goes with it become part of compulsory education and partly in humour as I knew how closed the powers in education were to putting any serious emphasis on tools that were genuinely useful for people in real life.

"Things can change!" I thought to myself. "And maybe I need to play a part in instigating that change" I reflected as I noticed I was adding an aspiration item to my list.

"Bye dad!" I said cheerily as I reached for my coat. Wendy had left an hour before.

"See you soon, son. Enjoy using your new tools in your toolbox" dad replied.

"Will do!" I called as I walked towards the door. "Thanks dad!"

"And thanks granddad!" I thought out loud as I stepped into the sunshine with a warm feeling inside.

ONWARDS...

Onwards simply means applying what you've discovered to work to get more of the outcomes you want. You can take what you've learned during inspeditions and expeditions and start applying it, testing it and refining it until you notice an improvement in your outcomes.

From what you learn during *inspeditions:*

1. Review what you discovered during an inspedition into a behaviour you do particularly well.

2. Take the things that make a difference (eg thinking voice, placement of the image, sounds, expectations etc) while at your best and apply them to an area where the additional resources could come in useful.

3. Check to see if changing your experience improved your outcomes. If it did, keep on doing it. If not, do something else.

From what you learn during *expeditions*:

1. Review what you discovered during your expedition into a behaviour someone you admire does particularly well.

2. Take the things that seem to make a difference for this person and apply them to a behaviour where you'd like the same success.

3. Check to see if adopting these behaviours improved your outcomes. If it did, keep on doing it. If not look again and do something else.

ACT "AS IF"

You can borrow other people's identities, expectations and beliefs and test them out for yourself.

If you'd like to exhibit the same successes as someone you admire then why not:

- Simply adopt their attitude, posture and approach to a situation and see what happens for you.

- If an aspect of their identity works, keep it and use it.

- If it doesn't work or it feels bad then discard it.

If you suspect that one of your beliefs may be hindering your ability to succeed then:

- Simply act "as if" you believed something that would support you in success

- If it works – keep it.

- If it doesn't work – do something else

UPWARDS – INTENSIFY WHAT WORKS

Upwards essentially means to intensify, amplify, magnify and build on things that work to test how they can work even better.

Got something that makes you feel great? Then:
- Imagine turning up a dial until it feels even better
- You can turn this dial up and down whenever you want

If your thinking voice is louder when you're at your best then:
Discover what happens when you make it louder still
- If it improves the experience keep making it louder
- If it doesn't then do something else

And above all else – commit to continuous improvement. Take your high achievement onwards and upwards. Keep testing, discovering, and noticing what works and you'll be surprised how easily you can achieve all you ever wanted.

The end...

(I lie – it was just the beginning!)

ABOUT THE AUTHORS

Tony Burgess and Julie French are committed to providing high quality coaching and training for people who are keen to become high achievers in their own right.

They are the founding directors of the Academy of High Achievers Ltd, *www.aha-success.com*, which was set up specifically for people who want to take their performance from excellent to outstanding through achieving massive and audacious goals.

To contact the authors email them at *jfrench@aha-success.com* or *tburgess@aha-success.com*

THE ACADEMY OF HIGH ACHIEVERS

The Academy of High Achievers Ltd is a dynamic, creative organisation that was set up to assist success-hungry people to launch themselves to new heights of excellence in their personal and professional performance.

There is a wide range of unique residential achievement programmes on offer to launch those who are genuinely looking for a giant leap forward in their lives.

The programmes include our hugely popular NLP Practitioner and Master Practitioner programmes and our flagship 'Ignite' events.

The Academy's Corporate Coaching programmes are specifically designed to enable people to discover and deliver their personal best, which will bring real tangible benefits to themselves and the organisation in which they work.

For more information about the Academy of High Achievers' success programmes, visit *www.aha-success.com* or phone +44 1785 716683 or +44 1785 255231

THE SUCCESS TOOLBOX

Great success books can be found at www.BookShaker.com

A few of the books that have inspired us over the years include:

'The one minute Millionaire' by Mark victor Hansen and Robert Allen

'Manifest your Destiny' by Wayne W Dwyer

'Synchrodestiny' by Deepak chopra

'Abundance in Action' by Michael Reitz

'Think and Grow Rich' by Napoleon Hill

'The Magic of Believing' by Claude M Bristol

'Creative Visualisation' by Shakti Gawain

'The Alchemist' by Paul Coelho

'The Celestine Vision' by James Redfield

'Awakening the Giant Within ' by Anthony Robbins

'Unlimited Power' by Anthony Robbins

Heart of the Mind by Connirae and Steve Andreas

Trance- formations: Neuro-Linguistic Programming and the Structure of Hypnosis by John Grinder and Richard Bandler

Introducing NLP by Joseph O'Connor and John Seymour

Frogs into Princes by Richard Bandler and John Grinder

The User's Manual For the Brain by Bob Bodenhamer and L Michael Hall

Challenging Belief Systems with NLP by Robert Dilts

The NLP Coach by Ian McDermott and Wendy Jago

Printed in the United Kingdom
by Lightning Source UK Ltd.
103481UKS00001B/490-528